Enlightened Women ~ Enlightened You

Journal

Enlightened Women ~ Enlightened You

Welcome! You are holding a journal, a gift, that was inspired by Archangel Michael, and was created as a supplement for the Enlightened Women ~ Enlightened You Summit. Each speaker from the summit is represented here in these pages, as are channeled messages from Divine Mother, Archangels Michael, Raphael, and Gabriel. There is room for you to share your thoughts, questions, and outrageous possibilities among the quotes. Grab your favorite beverage, settle in and join us!

If you are new to the summit, have you ever asked yourself these questions?
- How can I use divine guidance to survive and thrive through life's difficult challenges?
- How can I find and step into my soul's calling?

We did too!

Join an amazing group of women for a 31-day online summit called Enlightened Women ~ Enlightened You. Registering is as easy as signing up. You will then receive access to 31 spirit-led, inspiring videos. Join us and hear real women… living real lives… walking in Spirit. Welcome home. Take our hands. Let us walk beside you on your journey.

EnlightenedWorld.online/Enlightened-Women-Enlightened-You

Sincerely,

Dr. Ruth Anderson
EnlightenedWorld.online

Thank you to our Sponsors of Enlightened Women ~ Enlightened You Summit

ShaRon Rea

Champion for Outstanding Family Relationships, author, speaker, and owner of **TheWholeFamilyCoaching.com**, works with clients helping them live together with love, respect and cooperation. Join her global movement of **No Judgment. Just Love.**® to inspire us all to live together with unconditional allowance…one courageous action at a time.

ShaRon Rea
Champion for Outstanding Family Relationships
TheWholeFamilyCoaching.com

Founder of the Global Movement *No Judgment. Just Love.*®
NoJudgementJustLove.com

Founding Corporate Member of World Kindness USA
WorldKindness.org

Karen Palmer

Globalkindness Going Viral is a movement of moments which unites individuals, organizations, and communities to help co-create a kinder, more compassionate, and peaceful world that works for all. Join us at **GlobalKindnessTV.org**

Karen Palmer
Kindness Educator
Globalkindness Going Viral
Founder | Puppy Love Revolution

GlobalKindnessTV.org/Dream

Enlightened Women ~ Enlightened You
Summit Speakers

Debbie N. Goldberg	DebbieNGoldberg.com
Sheri Leigh Myers	MyAngelPrayer.com
Rebecca Hall Gruyter	YourPurposeDrivenPractice.com
Kristy Bright	KristyBright.com
Linda Patten	Dare2LeadWithLinda.com
Anümani Santos	AnumaniSpeaks.com
Olivia Parr-Rud, MS	OliviaPR.com
Sue Broome	SueBroome.com
Linda Dierks	SpinStrawtoGoldNow.com
Ivana Vozzo Morano	Facebook: Ivana.VozzoMorano
Stacie Harder	Facebook: Stacie Harder
Dr. Heather Harder	HeatherHarder.com
Pamela Olivia Brown	PamelaOBrown.Wordpress.com
Nancy Tarr Hart PhD	WalkingWisdom.life
Keleena Malnar	KeleenaMalnar.com
Debbie Garcia	Facebook: Spirituality Gone Wild
ShaRon Rea	NoJudgmentJustLove.com

Enlightened Women ~ Enlightened You
Summit Speakers

Niobe Weaver	Facebook: Songlight Niobe Weaver
Sommer Joy Ramer	Facebook: Sommer Joy Ramer
Sylvia Angelica Ferrero	BodySoulReboot.com
Mira Rubin	YourCoreConnection.com
Anayah Joi Holilly	AngelHeartRadio.com
Rebecca Abraxas	RebeccaAbraxas.com
Karen Palmer	GlobalKindnessTV.org
Carol Anne Cross	Facebook: Carol Anne Cross
Sharon Cryan	FoodNerdMeals.com
Karen D. Anderson	AskKarenAnderson.com
Monica Augustine	Energia-TransformYourLife.com
Ilina Ivana	Ilina Ivana / IlinaIvana.com
Neelam Minocha	NeelamMinocha.energy
Sheryl Glick	SherylGlick.com
Camille DeSalme	CamilleDeSalme.com
Teri Angel	AngelSpeakers.com
Victoria Friedman	VistarFoundation.org

May it be with the blessings of God
the universe, Divine Mother,
Archangel Michael, Archangel Gabriel,
and Archangel Raphael, that you,
beloved of God,
is anointed with love, light and blessings,
to step further into your role of sacred being. This
blessing is bestowed upon you
such that you and all souls
will be transformed through love and light.
May every action taken and every word
be said for the highest good of your growth,
Divine purpose, and for all involved.
May you always seek guidance and counsel
when you are unsure of your way.
In love and light, Amen

*Friendship... that one friend you can count on to let you be you,
to share yourself and laugh with.
That one friend that makes you feel you are home. That is love.
Find that friendship, that love, in the beauty that surrounds you.
Find that friendship in nature while you are walking in the field at night,
in the light of the moon, in the stars.
We all belong on this planet together: nature, earth, moon, sun.
Find love in your heart to care for nature.*

Find love and joy in each other.

~Divine Mother~

So we can choose to engage with someone, or we can choose to turn away and allow them to have their journey, even though we don't understand why they are living that kind of life.

We want them to live a better life of happiness and joy and health and vitality, but they have the right and the choice to live. And it will not be good for us to be in the energy of someone who is too far away from our path of learning to live in positivity and joy, and action for good too.

So we have to allow them to find their own way.
I always ask spirit to help them.

~ Sheryl Glick ~

Become engaged with your life.
Be your own creator.
At this moment, what are your
thoughts delivering to you?

~ Linda Dierks ~

You, fully awakened, are more powerful than all the
known technology currently available on this planet.
No crystals, gadgets, or gizmos are required.
All you have to do is trust and act in your greatness.

~ Dr. Heather Harder ~

I'm finding that the more I'm willing to show who I am,
it's like the Divine orchestrates the moments when the deeper
conversations with others can happen.

~ Anümani Santos ~

Be creative using vibrant, joyful life.
Feel and love deeply.
Live in color. Live through color.
Be brave and find your voice.
Sing with all your glory.
Don't just feel passionately,
but exude passion.
Let your passion push yourself to the edge,
which then gives you a
new edge to push toward.

~ Archangel Gabriel ~

What if we were so centered and balanced that we were able to see our
dog having a behavior "hiccup" with recognition of
how far they've come, instead of judgment or irritation?
Can you imagine how that energy would radiate to them,
causing organic, beautiful, radical change?

~ Kristy Bright ~

Be Willing to be Seen

Be willing to be seen on the same
level you want to serve.
If they cannot see you,
If they cannot hear you,
then you cannot help those who
need you most.
Be easy to find.

~ Rebecca Hall Gruyter ~

I kind of knew that there was some one always guiding me,
because every time I was in a predicament,
or in a situation that I could not handle,
I felt that there was someone always with me.

~ Ivana Vozzo Morano ~

Just as the stars are always in existence,
even when we can't see them, we are always standing in divine light,
even when we can't feel it.

~ Dr. Ruth Anderson ~

Rise up! You need to stand tall.
We have prepared you for this,
for this work.
You don't get to stay small.
The world needs you.

~ Archangel Raphael ~

Every choice brings awareness and possibility.
Every sound you make does too!
Sing out the heart sound "ah."
What awareness do you gain in the body?
Does it feel open or closed? What thoughts arise?
Does life force feel stuck or flowing through you?

~ Rebecca Abraxas ~

Life is a challenge.
It's how we adapt to the challenge
that makes us who we are.
In order for us to reach our goals,
We need to reach out and expand our
horizons.
We must continue to grow, and release
our stored knowledge.
We knew it when we returned.
It's now time to let it out, so we can
continue our journey.

~ Carol Anne Cross ~

Each of us is here with a call to be extraordinary,
to boldly embody our dreams and fulfill
our unique mission and purpose.
In serving a vision that's bigger than ourselves,
we naturally expand into unimagined capability,
soaring beyond perceived limitation and attachment
and into an uncharted realm of possibility,
freedom and magic.

~ Mira Rubin ~

Merge your heart with the cosmic heart... let it wrap around you and
fill you with unconditional love. No one externally can complete us.
We complete ourselves by building ourselves up from within.
When we are complete in ourselves, we meet people who
are also whole and complete in themselves.
Fill the cracks in your hearts... with cosmic love... it will never let you down.

~ Neelam Minocha ~

*Look around you and be inspired by the colors, not once,
but many times a day. There is healing in the leaves,
the grasses, and the waters of the ocean.
Inhale the color; let it flow through you.
Exhale to renew the flow and send it positively
out to the world so others can heal.*

~ Archangel Gabriel ~

Believe it or not practicing gratitude, has helped a lot with fears, at least it's helped me. Do this very frequently.

When you write down the journaling, I always suggest to people that should be journaling. And sometimes in the journal you can put something you cannot express verbally.

~ Ilina Ivana ~

Who Am I?

*I am cosmic consciousness...
an ebb and flow,
like the River Thames,
over memories, under desires,
and to possibilities.*

*Reflecting back to the world
its unknown magnificence,
I stop at nothing
to wash away moss and muck
collected from clashing experiences.*

*I am you...
manifested from love,
becoming whole again.*

~ Pamela Olivia Brown ~

Go to the forest and listen to the silence.
The Forest Angels have a message for you.
Quiet your mind and you will hear their wisdom...
Discover hidden truths in the rustling of the leaves.
Restore your soul through the rhythm of the babbling brook.
Feel your inner guidance align with the subtle shifts in the wind.
Embrace the Angels of the Forest.

~ Olivia Parr-Rud, MS ~

Intention

Intention is the Vibration of Creation. What am I creating with a focused intent in my silent thoughts or spoken words? Do I really wish to manifest that for myself or another? Hmm, I must remember,
I am always dancing with Creation!

~ Niobe Weaver ~

Don't limit my abilities, my power, by what you think I am capable of doing.
If you don't call on me, then you will never know what I can do.

There are a multitude of angels waiting to love you,
waiting to help.
You don't have to rely on yourself.

~ Archangel Michael ~

Finding love and joy within your body is part of
our divine journey.
Your body is a gift that you chose before coming to Earth;
she is your temple and guidance system...
always trust, honor, and celebrate your divine physical self.
How do you show your body your love and appreciation?

~ Stacie Harder ~

Life happens for you- not to you.

When life happens "to" you, you feel powerless and defeated.
(Something is taken away.) You're a victim of your circumstances.

But, when you can see life as a gift, then every event that happens
can be viewed as a package you are excited to open!
(Something is given.) You are the master of your fate, the captain of your soul.

~ ShaRon Rea ~

Oftentimes, great ideas come into your head.
If you don't act on them, it's like They go, "Oh, well,
she's not interested," and they move on.

Six months, a year later, when you see a book or a course,
you think, "I thought of that."

And it's like Spirit says to you, "Well, yeah, you did,
but you didn't take action on it.
So we sent it to somebody who would."

~ Linda Patten ~

Go into silence daily, connect to who you are at your Core,
at the DNA vibrational God/Goddess level.
This feeling, this knowing you will tap in to, will be the energetic life force
of who you truly are,
who you have always been and whom you will be eternally.

~ Karen D. Anderson ~

That's the thing with calling in the angels every single day...
connecting to the divine every single day... opening your heart.
The more you do it, the more of a habit it becomes.

~ Sue Broome~

Most people do not know or feel the Creator's heart that resides within them.
It contains infinite and eternal love, joy and peace.
Find it in the quiet stillness of meditation where you will come to know
that it holds the beauty of who you are and welcomes
the opportunity to be One with you.
You are an eternal flame of love that will never die.

~ Debbie N. Goldberg ~

When the angels give you
this big project,
the next thing you
have to do ...
must do... is just say,
"Angels, be with me on this."

~ Sheri Leigh Meyers ~

Life is a Doodle

When there is a break, a discontinuity
in the chatter of thoughts, there is a space of silence, a river of stillness
that opens a door to a secret, bottomless wellspring of expression
unknown to the mind. We create with and as that Source.

~ Victoria Friedman ~

It's been an interesting life.
And if I have a regret,
which I don't think that I really do have,
but if I have a regret, I would have to say that
I'm sorry that I waited so long to openly,
freely acknowledge and be honest about my
gifts and my spirituality.

~ Nancy Tarr Hart PhD. ~

> *My deeper awakening really empowered me to stand in my truth and be who I am, and I wasn't going to allow anyone to take that away from me anymore.*
>
> ~ Keleena Malnar ~

I am on this planet to bring forward the tools that
I've learned along this adventure we call life.

This beautiful glorious messy adventure,
that requires a new perspective almost on a daily basis.

My favorite part of life is teaching and learning new ways to spark
the g-vibe... new ways to improve and move forward in love.

~ Debbie Garcia ~

There is this place of curiosity and openness.
And, and I'm going to say deep, deep humility,
that I get to be a vessel for life as a vessel, an expression of God,
expression of life, whatever you want to call it,
whatever you want to believe in, but this isn't mine.
This life is a gift, this vessel, this body is an absolute gift.

~ Sylvia Ferrero ~

I never felt acceptable as a person. I felt that I was fundamentally broken and just wrong somehow. And it was in a way that I couldn't quite put my finger on I just knew that I was unlovable.

And of course, that then begins to generate a lot of acting out, a lot of anger, and misery. Through various times in my life, of course, I've had happiness, great happiness as well. But underlying that there was this pushing shove. You know, 'there's something wrong with you. No one's really going to love you.'

At the time, I thought that was a terrible thing. But of course, looking back now, I realized it was actually the opportunity for me to find my own wings and fly with them.

~ Anayah Joi Holilly ~

I think, "How can I start to be kind and generous to myself," and then that will ripple out to the person that I'm talking to, to the situation that I'm in. And then it's all about having compassion. And compassion and kindness always start in your own heart.

~ Karen Palmer ~

Give thanks often… just slow down and be in that moment
and think twice before you eat. And even if it's a split second
of gratitude, you're going to change your physiology,
you're going to digest the food better,
and you'll be able to assimilate the nutrients better.

~ Sharon Cryan ~

We have so much more capacity than I think we realize sometimes of what we're capable of really being in our lives.

~ Sommer Joy Ramer ~

It's a natural and healthy thing to acknowledge anger at feeling violated, being violated, not being treated fairly. And really wounded. Those types of abuses and experiences can wound somebody for their entire life. And if you're not conscious, you can really stay stuck in it.

So forgiveness has just been monumental. It's just mandatory. To learn how to do it and to muster up courage, really. It takes courage to forgive.

~ Monica Augustine ~

Some people say we're even, we're connected; and we may be.
But that presumes separation and I'm not even sure
that separation is true.

I have this sense we're all one thing; that there is no separation.
So there's no need for connection. It's just all one thing.

~ Camille DeSalme ~

I don't choose to go to any of the low vibration energy of fighting or struggle. It's just the journey is putting one foot in front of the other, handling one moment at a time.

And that's all we can do.

You know, you can't look forward. You can't look back; you can only handle the exact moment that you're in right now.

~ Teri Angel ~

Welcome to Enlightened World

Dr. Ruth Anderson is an award-winning, international best-selling author and founder of Enlightened World. Believing that spirit workers are often isolated and distracted from sharing their gifts, Dr. Anderson created Enlightened World. Enlightened World Online and Enlightened World Network serve to support lightworkers in building their professional visibility so they can share their talents with the world, at a time when it is desperately needed. Enlightened World also provides spiritually transformative articles, podcasts, courses, and summits to promote personal growth and support the good of the collective.

Please check out: **Enlightened World.online**
Enlightened World Network: **EnlightenedWorld.online**
YouTube: **bit.ly/33CyX3P**
Facebook: **Facebook.com/EnlightenedWorldNetwork**

Made in the USA
Columbia, SC
15 September 2019